HOW TO PLAN A
SUCCESSFUL
AUTHOR BOOK SIGNING

KATHY MASHBURN

Copyright © 2014 by Kathy W. Mashburn

Copyright © 2014 Cover Art by CreateSpace

Copyright © 2014 - Brooke Grant Photography

ALL RIGHTS RESERVED. Any unauthorized reprint or use of this material is prohibited. No part of this book may be reproduced or transmitted in any form or by any means, electronic or mechanical, including photocopying, recording, or by any information storage and retrieval system without express written permission from the author/publisher.

Published, May, 2014

How to Plan a Successful Author Book Signing is written based on the author's personal experience and success at her own book signing for *A Birthday Clown for Archer*. It is not meant to be an authority for planning events, nor is it a claim of expertise. It is a simple guide on how to go about planning your own event to put your books in the hands of readers.

http://www.KathyMashburn.com

Contents

Introduction 6
The Type of Event 9
Set the Date 12
The Venue 13
Announcements 16
The Invitation 17
Media Kit 20
Public Speaking Opportunities 22
Online Resources 24
Decorations 24
Activities 25
Mindy the Clown and Me 26
Favors and Giveaways 27
Logistics and Setup 28
Meet and Greet Every Guest 31
Coloring Activities 32
Face Painting 33
Reading Time and Entertainment 37
Sign, Sign, and Sign 41
Other Things to Consider 44

About Me 45

Have Fun 46

Thank you! 47

Request Additional Information 47

"From an early age, I have had a unique sense-of-self and a determined and entrepreneurial spirit. These qualities and opportunities to design and plan a variety of events, including weddings, baby showers, parties, and gatherings in the workplace for my family and friends over the years has given me the experience and expertise needed to plan, organize, and host my own successful book signing events.

My creativity and passion for designing special events for myself and others has never dulled. Planning events well have earned me a credible reputation of being a planner of choice for style savvy and budget conscious clients."

How to Plan a Successful Author Book Signing is written based on my personal experiences and success at my book signing for *A Birthday Clown for Archer*. It is not meant to be an authority for planning events, nor is it a claim to expertise. Hopefully, you will take away something from my experience that is helpful when planning your own events.

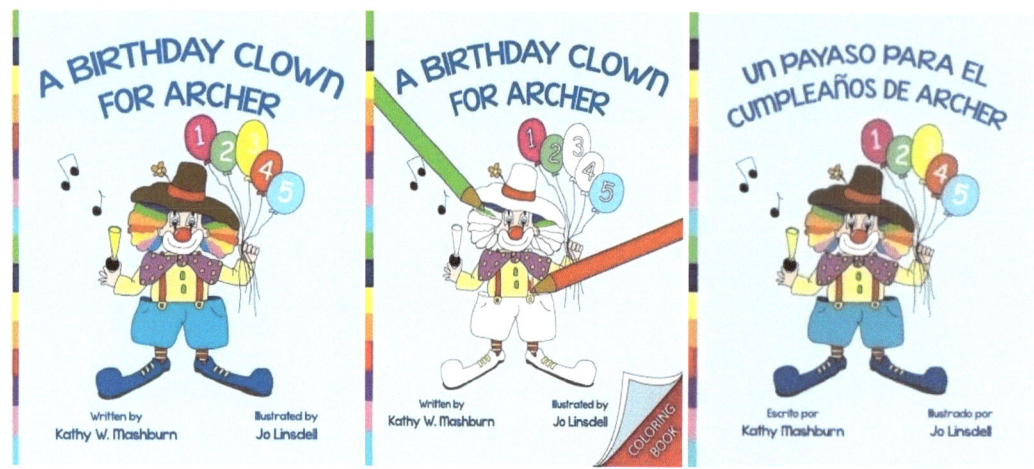

Available in English, Spanish, Kindle, and Coloring Book Editions

JUST THE FACTS

"A Birthday Clown for Archer" is written by
Kathy Mashburn and illustrated by Jo Linsdell
of Rome, Italy, and is available at
http://www.amazon.com, or by visiting
http://www.KathyMashburn.com, or
http://www.JoLinsdell.com.

Introduction

Imagine you've written a book and it has just been published! You are very excited and eager to spread the happy news, so you set out to organize a celebration to announce your book's release. The problem is you quickly get bogged down in the details and work that must be done to plan and host a successful book signing.

It's your book signing, so shouldn't you be spending your time celebrating with your readers and guests instead of working on the details? That's the purpose for me writing this simple "how to" book. It is also the result of me sharing information on the subject in response to the regular requests I receive from other authors, writers, illustrators, bloggers, and friends.

In *How to Plan a Successful Author Book Signing,* you will learn about the kinds of things I do and a host of other things I take into consideration when designing and planning my own events. There is countless ways for one to celebrate and promote their work as a writer. It is my hope you will find a few of my best practices useful. For me, a successful book signing is an essential and rewarding component to celebrate my writing endeavors and to build my personal author branding. I find book signings to be a lot of fun, and I absolutely love planning them. After reading *How to Plan a Successful Author Book Signing,* I hope you will too.

It's my belief every event should capture a personal style and be appealing to a targeted audience. What I mean by this is if you are the author of a children's book, like me, your event should be designed around children. This simple concept applies to any genre you may enjoy writing.

When planning an event like a book signing for a children's book, you must keep in mind children cannot transport themselves and most likely will not have jobs, so you must be sure the event appeals to parents, grandparents, and other adults who will be transporting them to an event.

If you can keep these two thoughts in mind when planning your book signing, your guests will be more likely to remember your memorable celebration.

Because I enjoy planning events of all sizes and for most occasions, I sometimes offer my services to others in my local area to provide full or partial event planning, starting with a FREE consultation and an agreement to coordinate the event on the special day.

From elaborate events to festive parties, including book signings, I am dedicated to making every event special in every way possible down to the smallest details when I am privileged to assist in the design and planning.

The launch of your book is an important day and it should be a reflection of your personal style, desires, and needs. A successful signing should be a gratifying experience of you to meeting and greeting your audience.

While I understand the importance of perfection, the need for detail, and I am committed to the highest level of service and professionalism, I also pride myself in staying budget conscious to maximize the most bangs-for-the-buck in designing my own events and those for others.

To begin a plan for any type of event, I prefer to start with a simple list of things to consider, including the venue selection, a list of needed vendors, invitations, advertisements, music, table décor, room décor, furniture setup, party favors, tableware and linen, menus, programs, entertainment, rental equipment and coordination of the day.

My first priority is to create an experience that is beautiful, unique, and memorable for my readers. I want my guests to find my events to be warm and inviting, so that they enjoy themselves and are likely to attend subsequent events on my behalf. In order to do this, I must first determine every need, including who the book signing is geared toward or who is my specifically targeted audience. Then I determine ways to meet the needs I have determined.

Ultimately the planning of details should be such that it allows you or another to focus on the simple joy and fun of the celebration.

At this point, I would to reiterate the information included in this book is a recount of my personal experiences when planning my book signing for *A Birthday Clown for Archer*. I hope you will find it beneficial to you when planning your own.

The Type of Event

Whether you are planning a book signing or other type of event, you should start by asking a few basic questions like when will you plan to hold your event? Who is your audience, or whom do you expect to attend? What is it you wish to accomplish? Why are you holding the event? What are your goals and how will you accomplish them? When you know the answers to these questions, you can drill down a little deeper to answer more specific questions like will the event be for a few guests or many guests? Will the event be held indoors or outdoors? What kinds of materials and supplies will you need at the event (i.e., tables, chairs, balloons, etc.)?

As you already know from the introduction, my event was to hold a book signing. So let me begin by sharing with you in the remainder of this book the details and considerations I made to ensure a successful event.

Set the Date
When choosing a date and time for your event be sure to set them based on what will be appropriate for your audience. For example, I set the times for my recent book signing for *A Birthday Clown for Archer* from10:00 a.m. to 2:00 p.m. (Eastern Standard Time)

because it's my belief most adults prefer to attend events that are neither too early nor too late, especially when they are for children. My most successful events have been set to last a minimum of two hours, but generally no more than three. Of course, if you experience hundreds of guests showing for your book signing you should be flexible in extending the scheduled time, making certain the host or venue is flexible as well. Don't worry about this too much because you will know or get a feel for when the event should end based on the attendance. It's a good thing when more guests than you expect come to join your celebration and to buy your books.

On the other hand, if I were a romance writer I might choose to set a date and time for a Saturday evening event and include little black dresses, fresh flowers, chocolates, and cocktails in my planning.

Again, as you begin the planning process for your event, you should always take into consideration first the targeted audience and the genre you have written.

The Venue

Selecting a venue can be tricky. First of all, the venue should be one that makes sense based on the topic or genre of your book. Also, as mentioned earlier, a venue should be flexible in the time scheduled, so that you could accommodate an extended time if one is needed. At my event, The Ice Castle (a local ice cream shop) was the perfect venue for me to introduce *A Birthday Clown for Archer* to my readers. Not only was it a fun place for children to come, it was a great place for adults to have a quick and delicious lunch while their children participated in the festivities I had planned for the day. I made sure to include this information in my marketing materials to prepare my guests and to support the shop and its owner.

Like my earlier example, a romance writer would most likely want to choose a venue like a nice restaurant or a local winery while keeping their adult audience in mind.

The point, I'm trying to make is to be creative. Make your venue choice based on the genre of your book and your audience.

A couple examples I can think of is an author who writes western books might choose a saddle club or local rodeo event to hold his or her signing at, and may include props like cowboy hats and hay bales to sit on.

A children's author who plans to celebrate the release of a new book about Christmas will find it beneficial to plan an event near Santa's workshop in the mall. An event in the mall would be a great opportunity to introduce a Christmas book because countless children and parents visit the mall frequently during the holidays to see the big Jolly guy in the red suit. If you can arrange to set up an event near him, then you will automatically have an opportunity to meet and greet customers and to sell your Christmas book.

Now that you have selected and secured a venue or host for your event, you must determine what they will or will not provide. For examples, you will need tables and chairs. Don't assume they are provided and don't assume anything else. This part of the planning requires you to be really detailed about all things decided on from here on out. I have held events where I have provided everything and other events where I provided very little to nothing. What you provide will depend on the agreement you have with the venue or host. Be prepared! Ask questions about everything you can think of and then take notes on the details.

What I mean is if the venue provides tables and chairs for you to use, make sure they have enough tables and chairs to meet your needs. If the venue offers to provide a drink station, find out what they will serve and if there's a cost to you for cups and sodas. If the venue says they will promote your event, and then ask them how. Again, be specific when asking what exactly they will plan to do, so you can determine if you should do other things in conjunction with their efforts or should you do most of spreading the word yourself. Offer to share any promotional materials you are planning to do yourself like flyers, brochures, rack cards, etc.

Finally, once you have chosen your venue make an extra effort to get to know the owner and those staff members (if you don't know them beforehand) who will be working on the day of your event.

The photo below is of the owner of the Ice Castle, Inc, Ms. Cindi Deal Brown and two of her staff members Gina and Brittney and of course Mindy the Clown who I had hired to provide entertainment during my book signing. As you can see in the photo, I made certain to include them in the festivities and I provided them with (FREE) themed t-shirts to wear during the event. This went a long way to gain their willingness to help me sell books and to service my guests above and beyond what was expected. The shirts were a simple gesture of thanks and were much appreciated by all as you can see by their radiant smiles.

Announcements

When designing invitation, announcements, and other marketing materials for my events, I like to create them myself by using a computer and Microsoft Publisher. I begin with creating a draft of what I would like them to say, making sure to include the details of where, when, why, and what will occur. Being creative is one of my strongest suits so I enjoy designing most of my promotional materials. I also find it to be the most economical means for me to produce quality materials.

Once my designs are finished, I send the final products (postcards, flyers, business cards, rack cards, banners, etc.) to a local printer in my community for processing. This serves two purposes as the owner of the shop graciously posts promotional flyers in his store windows to help me get the word out and it builds my rapport in the community which enhances my efforts to build a successful author brand. Giving back to your community by volunteering and supporting your local merchants is never a bad thing, so take advantage of every opportunity you can.

I would be remiss to move on from this section without first emphasizing the importance of designing uniform materials. What this means is you should have a common theme or thread for all of the materials you plan to use. My business cards are a great example of this because they were designed to be a reflection of my website, which was professionally done using a backdrop of black, white, and silver. I hope you will visit http://www.kathymashburn.com to see what I mean. Along with business cards, I have a couple banners in different sizes that were designed in the same professional manner. The idea is to create uniform materials that can be used anywhere and that are effective in building your personal brand. That's why I have designed a slew of "generic materials" that are suitable for use anytime regardless of the type of event or genre of a book. Don't misunderstand; you will always need "event specific" materials as well, but a stock of professional materials for any occasion is a smart idea.

The Invitation

Designing invitations is one of my favorite things about planning a book signing, or other type of event. Invitations can be designed and economically produced for any occasion including formal affairs, whimsical parties, classic gatherings, and traditional events.

For my book signing for *A Birthday Clown for Archer* I wanted an invitation that said, "Fun!" I also needed an invitation that kids would relate to and one that would convey to parents or other adults that children would love attending my event.

Since almost every child's party I have ever attended has included an array of festive balloons, I felt sure an invitation decorated with them would help me to communicate my message clearly to my intended audience of children. I was confident children and parents would assume where there was a clown there would be balloons. So, the invitation I selected had sculpted or twisted balloons on its front which was perfect for my occasion, especially since the entertainment I planned to provide included a clown to sculpt balloons for my guests.

To begin creating my personal invitations, I first do a quick search of the Internet to look for free and downloadable templates. Online you can find countless themes and designs to choose from and most templates are easy to use to print invitations. Some templates have fixed designs that cannot be changed (other than text), but other templates allow you to create your own designs by uploading clip art, photos, graphics and font sizes and styles.

Of course you can always start with a blank page in any size to create your own invitations using programs like Microsoft Word, Microsoft Publisher, or Adobe Design, Photoshop, or Illustrator. With a little practice you will quickly master how to create beautiful and fun invitations for any occasion.

When printing my own invitations, I prefer to use a heavy cardstock and size them to fit a standard envelop. On occasion, I need invitations that will not be stuffed into envelopes for mailing. When this is the case, invitations are sized the same as stand or oversized postcards. This makes it easy for me to apply postage and drop them in the mail quickly. My personal rule of thumb is to mail my printed invitations to my family, friends, and other guests at least two weeks prior to the event. Digital invitations are just as easily created by saving your invitation design as a PDF and emailed to your online guest list and posted on your website about two weeks prior to the event as well. Digital invitations can also be resent a few days prior to the event as a gentle reminder to attend.

If you choose, you can purchase both invitations and envelopes at very reasonable prices from many sites on the Internet. Three of my personal favorites are http://www.VistaPrint.com, http://www.123Print.com, and http://www.OrientalTrading.com. Each of these online printing services offers economical and beautiful design templates and envelopes. In fact, the invitation you see below from my book signing was printed by http://VistaPrint.com. These printing services, and others like them, offer not only invitations but a host of other marketing and promotional materials that can be coordinated for most any occasion.

The last thing I want to share in this section is to remind you to be specific when providing details about your event. Make certain you include the date, the time, the location, and your contact information, but also create excitement by including a note about any entertainment, refreshments, and favors and free giveaways. By doing this you will increase the likelihood your readers will remember your upcoming event and mark their calendars not to miss it.

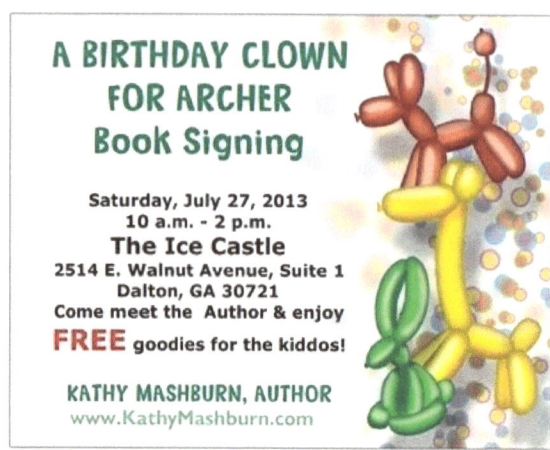

Media Kit

Once you have defined all of the details about your event you will want to spread the word as fast as you can and to help you do that you should consider creating a Media Kit to add to your tool belt of resources. A Media Kit can be simple or complex, but ideally, either one should answer the same basic questions discussed earlier in the ***Determine the Type of Event*** section. You must make sure to include complete details about your book, or product, or your purpose, which should capture the interest and attention of various media groups. You must be certain you know the answers to who, what, when, where, why, and how before you ever disseminate a media kit to others, and you must be able to communicate this information on demand as opportunities occur. This is not a part of the process for planning events that you would want to be caught unprepared. You want to be noticed and you do not want to come across in the Media or to you audience as amateurish, unprofessional, or having a lack of knowledge about your product or service. Always be prepared before you spread the word by knowing exactly what you would say if caught off guard.

A media kit can be put together in any fashion based on your personal style and your purpose. For me, it works best to create a media kit for each of my individual books or projects. However, I also find it beneficial to have a "general" media kit to use to introduce myself; the genres I enjoy writing; and my social platforms and means of contact. A personal media kit should be more about you and less about your product or a combination of both. It is important for you to include the credentials you have that qualify you as an author or an expert on whatever subject matter you are providing media groups.

My media kit for *A Birthday Clown for Archer* included an information sheet to introduce the book, as well as an explanation as to why I had written a book about Coulrophobia (Clown-phobia). I provided the reader with a brief statement about my personal experiences of dealing with one of my daughter's fear of clowns. This made it real to my audience.

One of the first things I do is before this is preparing a Media Kit. In addition to invitations, I always spread the word through as many channels as possible, including school visits, public appearances, local Media, blogging, web visits, interviews, and word-of-mouth, etc. Photos of these kinds of activities are below.

Public Speaking Opportunities

Online Resources

Decorations

This was my easiest task. To decorate for my event, I simply purchased a jumbo roll of festive plastic table-cover to dress the tables in the shop and added several clusters of balloons as a centerpiece. I bought these materials at a local craft store the morning of the event.

Activities

Choose and plan activities to compliment your book. For mine, I hired a local clown, Mindy, to entertain the children with face painting, sculpted balloons, and simple magic tricks. By doing this I was certain children would come and fun would be had by all. After all most would agree when children have fun, Moms and Dads have fun! It was a strategy that worked well at my event. Locally you can find Mindy the Clown at funtimesandtunes@aol.com.

Mindy the Clown and Me

Favors and Giveaways

No event or party would be complete without party favors and giveaways, so I selected mine based on my audience and the genre of my book. It was very fitting to provide the children in attendance with free coloring pages, crayons, sculpted balloons, face painting, and a ticket for an ice cream cone. For adults, I held a random drawing each hour for a $10 gift certificate to the Ice Castle. This was a simple way for me to thank the shop owner and to support her business, while adding to my mailing list when guests signed up for the door prize drawings.

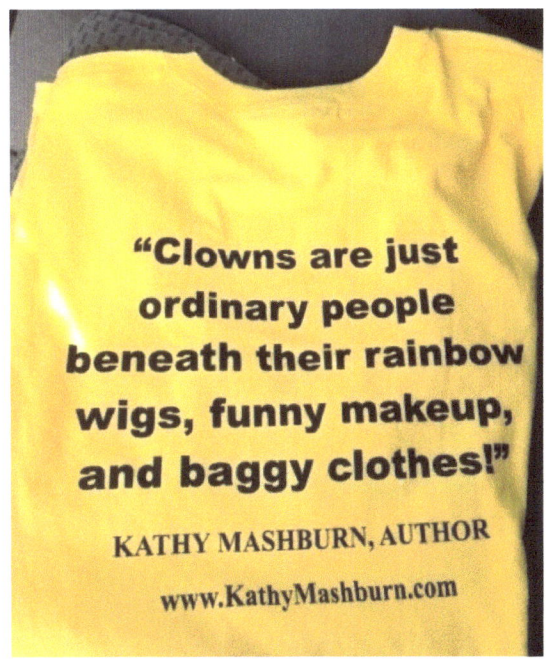

Logistics and Setup

Because I prefer to spend my time greeting my readers and signing my books, I asked a few of my family and friends to help me out. I set a table nearest the entry of the ice cream shop as the point-of-sale and there placed my two most talkative helpers. These two were extremely valuable as they promoted my books to everyone who stopped by to see me. They also managed the favors and door prize drawings, with the exception of ice cream tickets. Be certain those you choose to assist with this aspect of your signing are not shy. You want them to know every detail about your book and to communicate the details to the public with ease. At my event, I also asked these folks to sell special t-shirts I had designed to promote me and my author website. This was a little costly, but it went a long way in helping to build my personal brand and recognition. I also gave tees away to the staff of the Ice Castle and requested them to wear them during the event. They loved them and were more than accommodating to me and my guests.

Meet and Greet Every Guest

Coloring Activities

Face Painting

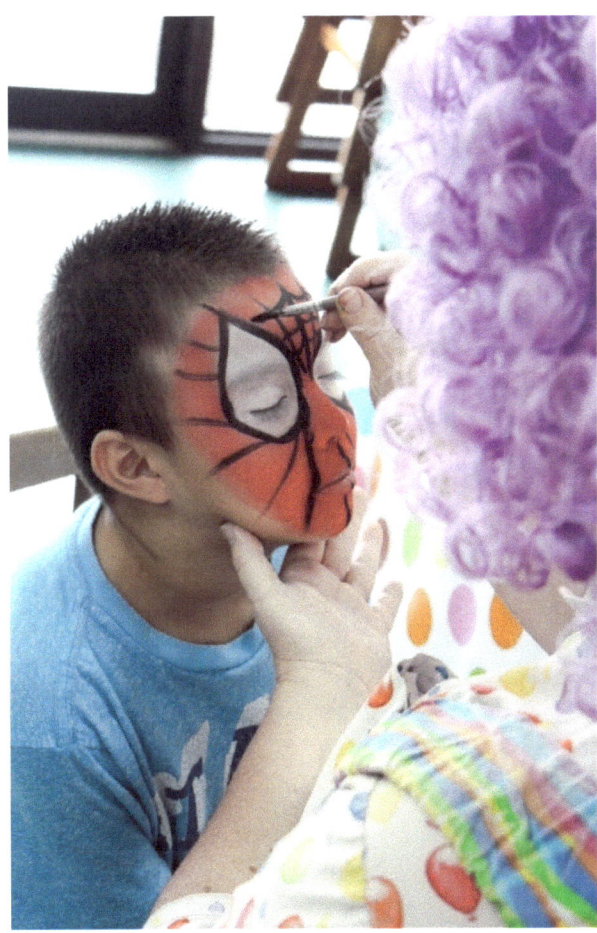

Reading Time and Entertainment

Near the center of the shop I placed a table for Mindy the Clown. This was the real point of fun for kids. I knew children would be excited to get a book and tee, but I also knew they would be doubly excited to meet Mindy. When you make plans to offer entertainment, be sure what you choose is relevant and that credible persons will carry out your ideas in a satisfactory manner. What I mean is if Mindy the Clown had said she could sculpt animal balloons, but then could only draw faces using a magic marker on round balloons the effect would not have been the same.

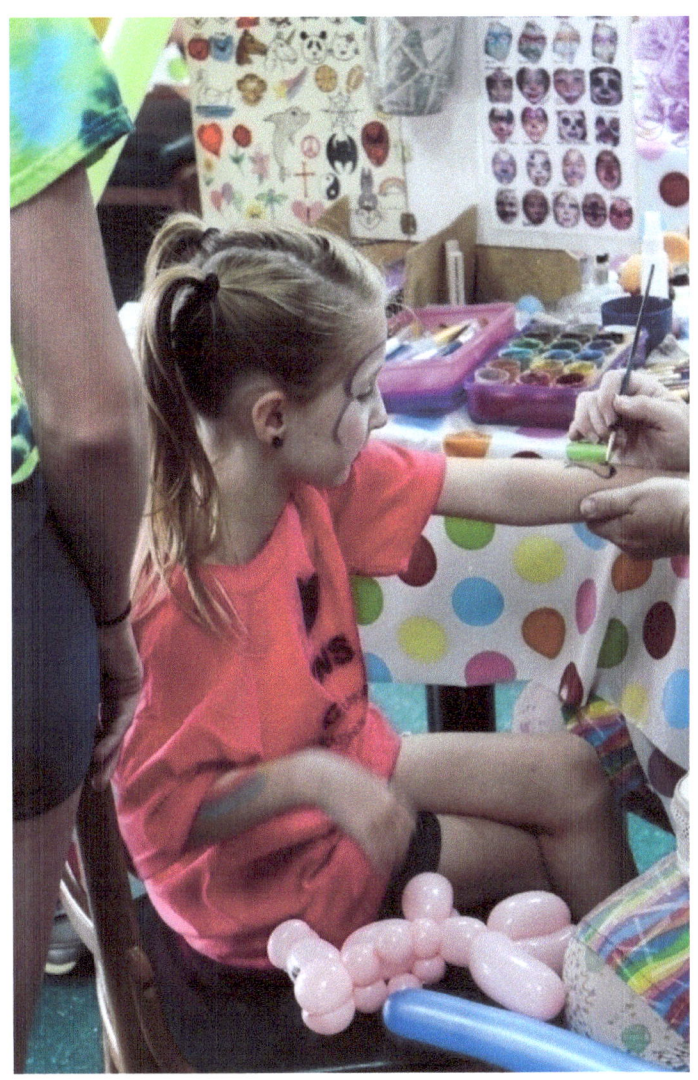

I settled myself at a table near Mindy, being careful not to be too close. I had a giant poster made of the cover of my book and posted a sign that read, "Meet the Author and Get Your Book Signed." Kids eagerly came over to ask for my autograph and to listen to me read the story aloud. I also took pictures with anyone who asked. Before a child left my station, I made sure to give each one a ticket for an ice cream cone. This alone made me a celebrity (Ha-ha)! When I was not busy, I would move to stand near Mindy to interact with the kids. We had balloon sword fights, we danced in a conga line around the shop, and we giggled over Mindy's magic and funny face paintings.

Sign, Sign, and Sign

Other Things to Consider

To complete the plans for my book signing, I employed the services of an inexpensive photographer to capture the special moments of the day. Remember when I said I would rather meet my readers and sign books than be bogged down with the details, well this was an example of exactly that. Having a photographer on hand guaranteed me lots of quality photos to use for future marketing and promotional endeavors. Besides, my guests loved it! It also allowed me to invite them to join my social platforms to see the photos taken at a later date. This grows my following and permits me to send personal messages of thanks to my guests a few days after the event. I am certain you will find this to be a wise investment worth making.

About Me

Although I enjoy writing across genres, I spend much of my time writing books for children. The stories I write are usually based on an awareness issue like the fear of clowns, or a disability concern like having prosthetic limbs or being blind. Of course, I also enjoy writing stories that are just simply FUNNY! It is my hope the books I write will engage children in a positive way, encouraging them to laugh, learn, and to stretch their imaginations.

Have Fun

Regardless of whether it is my book signing or another's event, I design my services to meet the needs based on an individual basis. I do not offer standard "packages" to choose from, nor do I actively promote myself as a planner. However, I never turn down an opportunity to assist others when possible. Because every event is unique, I take the time to listen carefully to your personal style and desires before designing a budgeted plan.

Thank you!

If you have purchased or downloaded this book or any of my other books available on Amazon.com, please take a moment to leave a short review. Reviews are an important part of promoting my work and growing my audience. I sincerely appreciate your feedback. To learn more about me or my work, please visit my website at http://www.KathyMashburn.com.

Remember, it's your party, so don't get bogged down in the details – JUST HAVE FUN!

Request Additional Information

To request additional information, write to me at P. O. Box 3962, Dalton, GA 30719.

www.ingramcontent.com/pod-product-compliance
Lightning Source LLC
Chambersburg PA
CBHW050902180526
45159CB00007B/2767